Wally Fawkes (Trog) is one of the most original and respected cartoonists of our time. Born in Canada in 1924, he came to England at the age of seven. After school in Sidcup, Kent, he won a scholarship to the Sidcup School of Art, his only formal art training apart from a brief spell at the Camberwell School of Art. He joined the *Daily Mail* in 1945, after he had been 'spotted' by Leslie Illingworth (his 'fairy godfather'), and in 1949 he created the comic strip *Flook* for the *Mail*. The succession of distinguished writers with whom he has worked on *Flook* includes Humphrey Lyttelton, Sir Compton Mackenzie, George Melly, Barry Norman and Barry Took. He now both writes and illustrates *Flook* himself.

Trog's career as a political cartoonist began in 1959 when he started doing a small weekly cartoon for *The Spectator,* and cartoons for *Private Eye* followed. Then came *The New Statesman* and *The Observer,* after which Trog drew daily political cartoons for the *Daily Mail.* He returned to *The Observer* in 1971 as its weekly political cartoonist, adding 'Mini-Trog', a small front-page cartoon on lighter news topics. At the same time, he drew a weekly full-page cartoon for *Punch,* a magazine to which he still contributes regularly, often drawing its cover.

In 1976, Trog was voted International Political Cartoonist of the Year by members of the International Salon of Cartoons, and in 1977 Cartoonist of the Year by Granada Television's 'What the Papers Say'.

To many, Wally Fawkes is also known as a brilliant jazz clarinettist. His musical career started with the formation of the George Webb Dixielanders in 1943, and he later broke away to join Humphrey Lyttelton's band, with whom he toured Britain and Europe. Both jazz and drawing have remained integral and complementary parts of his artistic life.

Due to circumstances beyond his control, Trog will not be
drawing a cartoon this week...

Punch, April 4, 1973

VAT replaces SET and Purchase Tax on April 1st

The World of Trog

of

Trog

Introduced by JAMES CAMERON

Robson Books

Editorial note
Captions in italics are reminders of the news items which prompted the cartoons; the
others belong to the drawings. Sources and dates are also given.

Key: DM = *Daily Mail*
   Obs = *Observer*

THE WORLD OF TROG FIRST PUBLISHED IN GREAT BRITAIN IN 1977 BY
ROBSON BOOKS LTD., 28 POLAND STREET, LONDON W1V 3DB.
COPYRIGHT (c) 1977 WALLY FAWKES.

Grateful acknowledgement is made to the proprietors of the *Daily Mail (Associated Newspapers
Group Ltd.), The Observer* and *Punch* for permission to use the cartoons appearing in this book.

ISBN 0 86051 020 4

Printed and bound in Great Britain by Redwood Burn Ltd., Trowbridge & Esher

Introduced by
JAMES CAMERON

It is a singular fact, or so it seems to me, that major political cartoonists, unlike troubles, almost always come singly. There is the occasional overlap, but the main rule is that you have a Partridge, then you have a Dyson, then you have a Low, and then you have a Vicky, but almost never do you have any of them at once. They do not, perhaps fortunately, arrive at their summit simultaneously. They are rare and occasional creatures, to be treasured as pearls of great price. The best of them are indeed pretty pricey, as they deserve to be. Of great and good cartoonists there is never a glut, and least of all today.

Following this law of apostolic succession, today is our time of the Trog.

Trog is of course Wally Fawkes, the tall thin chap with the glasses and the sceptical expression and the magical fingers. It never occurred to me to ask him whether he is from the seed of Guy Fawkes; it could be; he has the same iconoclastic impulses and a similar urge to pull the rug from under pretentious politicians. It might be worth serious consideration to institute a November day as Wally Fawkes Day, and burn Wallys instead of Guys. I know at least four public persons who would go along with that. A penny for the Wally? Some hopes.

I think Trog is by far and away the most compelling political cartoonist of our times. I am a pretty captious critic of cartoonists. It is a little known fact, thank God, that I was once one myself; indeed I once stood in for Osbert Lancaster while the master was away on diplomatic business, until I learned that good intentions were no substitute for talent. I had plenty of the first and little of the second. I retreated into words.

The gospel according to Wally 'Trog' Fawkes: 'You read the news and give yourself the subject-matter for the cartoon. You decide that this is the story of the week and you read all the papers. You begin to get feelings about it. Whose side are you on? Is this right? Is this fair? This is the sort of gut-feeling you have. You wait for the digestive phase, then with any luck the answer comes floating to the surface, and you start to draw.'

How simple: you start to draw.

It makes a difference if you know how.

Wally Fawkes went to the Sidcup School of Art, his only official training. He was a disciple of Leslie Illingworth, as who was not. Between them they influenced this wild colonial boy into a draughtsman of truly outstanding skill and impact. I would humbly say that Trog's *Punch* cover of Edward Heath in October 1974 is simultaneously a magnificent caricature and a very serious work of portraiture. I have (though in no circumstances must anyone tell Trog about it) got it stuck on my wall.

The political cartoonist's work is – like ours – evanescent. He draws for the moment, as we write for the moment. Yet there is a difference: the cartoonist cannot camouflage the lack of a direct or cogent idea in an embroidery of phrases, as we are so often obliged to; he cannot draw *round* the matter as we can with a bit of ingenuity write round the matter; with the political cartoonist it is there or it isn't. His work is for him who runs and reads; anything that needs more than a minute's analysis will miss the bus. That is why their job is more exacting than ours, which is saying something.

There are exceptions to this generality, of course; some cartoonists' work has an intrinsic fascination quite independent of its immediate message, or joke, or barb, or whatever. The best of Trog can be viewed and re-viewed over and again, as meaningful and valuable drawings. Trog has a style of great solidity and purpose; he may not pull it off every time but by gum you know he means it. He has not the elfin fluency of a Vicky or the mannered brushwork of a Low, but his work jumps out of the page in a way they would have envied. The only word that comes to mind is 'massive'. When Wally Fawkes describes Trog as 'a two-bottle-a-day' man (meaning Indian ink, naturally) it is almost credible, so dark and penumbral are the cartoons and so inescapably do they dominate every page that carries them.

He has the proper bitterness imperative for this craft. He is also, I would suggest, more of a fantasist then most, and certainly a more concentrated physical observer. His trick, when he feels like using it occasionally, is to limn the central, real character with great care and detail, leaving any stray anonymous chorus-characters as simplified blank symbolic faces. This is Trog-shorthand for the public facelessness, and powerlessness, and if the phrase makes Pseuds' Corner by and by it has my blessing.

I have said that Trog at his best is a supreme portraitist, with an excellent line in malice. Richard Nixon was of course a pushover, but he also did the best Gerald Ford in the business, and it cannot have been easy to have caught a countenance of such sublime emptiness and give it a kind of life it never had in reality. I don't think too much of his Margaret Thatchers, but then I try not to think too much of Margaret Thatcher either. He has an accurate bead on the Royals (I think he has done the lot of them for *Punch* at one time or another) but I would guess he has a latent gallantry (or maybe discretion) that draws a delicate frontier between satire and generosity.

The Trog *curriculum vitae* is set forth on another page. It is worth recalling, however, that he did not see the light in these shores – as what major cartoonist did? He originated not in New Zealand, like David Low, nor in Hungary-via-Berlin, like Vicky, but in Canada. This must have a meaning, though for the moment I cannot think what. (I am reminded of the fact, or the legend, that the surrender of Quebec was accepted by the first known caricaturist, Brigadier-General George Townshend, who took over after General Wolfe was killed. Could that be the answer?)

There must be many people who still know Trog, the celebrated commentator-in-line, as Wally Fawkes, the gifted jazz musician, as deft on the clarinet as on the page. Somebody must one day consider a thesis on the odd association of cartooning with music. Gilray was said to be no mean fiddler; Low's hobby was the piano; Vicky was such an addict that it was a rare evening indeed that did not find him at a symphonic concert; George Melly collaborated with Wally on his early *Spectator* cartoons. Discuss and analyse.

Anyhow, as a considerable artist in two fields, Wally 'Trog' Fawkes is our man. I am sufficiently impertinent to call him a friend of mine; he is sufficiently generous not to protest. I salute him and this book; may they both prosper forever.

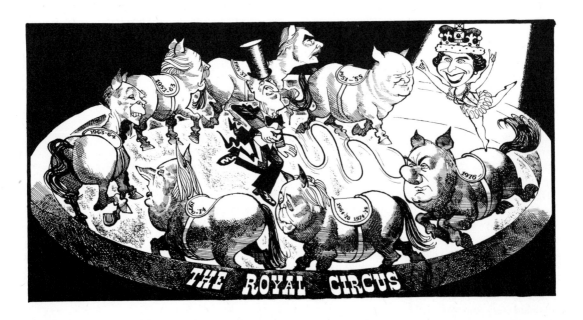

'I shouldn't pour his just yet…'   DM, May 5, 1969

Despite Labour Party split over change of leadership, forced resignation seems unlikely

DM, June 20, 1969

DM, Oct 30, 1969

DM, Jan 16, 1970

George Brown on last stage of Middle East fact-finding tour

Punch, May 12, 1971

How high this time?

Punch, July 21, 1971

Punch, Oct 13, 1971

Forward!

'So much for your advanced technology…'   Obs, Feb 20, 1972

10

Modern Times   Punch, Feb 16, 1972

opposite

Pompidou visit put off by miners' strike

Heath runs into opposition from Anti-Marketeers

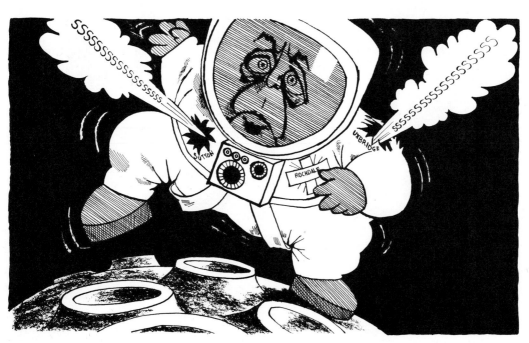

End of the Odyssey?   Obs, Dec 10, 1972

Last moon-shot coincides with Wilson's by-election set-backs

'Gentlemen, you don't make it very easy.'

Punch, Dec 20, 1972

Picking up another pilot   Punch, Jan 3, 1973

Britain joins EEC

Punch, May 30, 1973

Obs, June 11, 1973

'Couldn't be any worse than the other farces they have down there.'

Obs, Sept 23, 1973

Punch, Nov 28, 1973

...And in the morning he was still a frog.   Punch, Mar 6, 1974

Obs, April 14, 1974

Change of tune　　Obs, June 9, 1974
Renegotiating Britain's entry to the EEC

'Quickly, a new sabre, even if it's just to rattle!'   Obs, June 23, 1974

EEC Referendum victory for Wilson despite bid by Anti-Marketeer Tony Benn to lead Labour Party division

The Alchemists   Punch, Sept 25, 1974

Pre-election days...

Punch cover, Oct 9, 1974

Obs, Jan 25, 1976

Icelandic Prime Minister in London for talks on fishing limits

Obs, Feb 8, 1976

Allegations against Thorpe are raised in the Press

Obs, Feb 29, 1976

Russia accuses Mrs Thatcher of being a witch

Obs, May 9, 1976

Obs, Mar 28, 1976

Obs, July 4, 1976

Obs, July 11, 1976

*Newly-elected Liberal leader David Steel meets with
'sulky attitude' from Cyril Smith as Princess
Anne sets off for the Montreal Olympics*

Liberal leadership fight clashes with Wimbledon

Obs, Aug 29, 1976

The long hot summer of '76

The big drought, '76   Obs, Oct 3, 1976

Denis Howell brings drought to an end, but . . .

Obs, Oct 24, 1976

Another amazing turnaround   Obs, Nov 7, 1976

Woman missing overboard in Atlantic keeps afloat $2\frac{1}{2}$ hours before the Windsor Castle *turns round and sights her*

Obs, Nov 21, 1976

Obs, Dec 5, 1976

Obs, Feb 13, 1977

30

Obs, Feb 13, 1977

Joe Haines and Lady Falkender disagree over his published account of life at No. 10

'Apart from that, Mrs.Wilson, how did you enjoy the Cabaret?'

Mrs Thatcher denounces Russians while on visit to China

The Stripper   Punch, May 25, 1977

Punch cover, Nov 17, 1971

Punch cover, Sept 17, 1969

Punch cover, Mar 3, 1971

Punch cover, May 2, 1973

Obs, May 8, 1977

Punch, Jan 9, 1974

'Is it really true that one day all this will be mine?'

Jubilee number   Punch cover, April 6, 1977

Punch, April 28, 1971

DM, Feb 28, 1969

Upper Clyde Shipyards bankrupt

Enough Rope?   Punch, June 23, 1971

The Thaw   Punch, Mar 8, 1972

Tory dogma feels the heat

The Grand Masters   Punch, July 12, 1972

Government and TUC hold prices and incomes talks

Punch, Oct 4, 1972

Animal Farm
Big unions claim greater need

Punch, May 2, 1973

May Day '73

Pit Disaster   Punch, Nov 20, 1974

Miners' ballot rejects National Coal Board productivity pay scheme

Obs, July 4, 1976

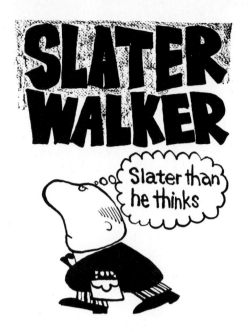

Obs, Sept 19, 1976

Downfall of Slater Walker Securities

Punch, Mar 9, 1977

Leyland Lemmings

Phase Three   Punch, May 4, 1977

opposite

'Each generation is judged, not merely for what it can
do for itself but for what it can do for the next' – from
The Case for Maplin

DM, Nov 29, 1968
Concorde featured on New Year commemoration stamp

Punch, Aug 1, 1973

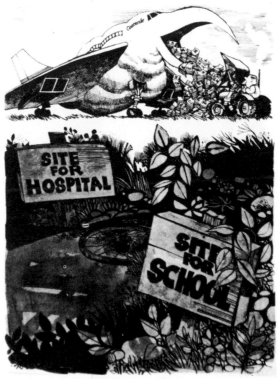

Punch, June 12, 1974

DM, Dec 10, 1969

Punch, Dec 6, 1972

Plight of the old age pensioners
at Christmas

'Sorry we've got to go, Mum, but he wants to see it in colour.'

Punch, Dec 4, 1974

Punch, June 16, 1971

DM, Mar 19, 1968

Vanessa Redgrave leads anti-Vietnam war demonstration

The Long Arm of the Law   Punch, Sept 8, 1971

Police renew call for capital punishment

Obs, Feb 22, 1976

Constable Exhibition opens after Tate Gallery buys pile of bricks

Obs, Mar 4, 1976

Obs, Oct 3, 1976

Ken Tynan's successor to Oh! Calcutta *opens*

'THE VERY IDEA—
WOMEN IN PRIESTS' CLOTHING!'

Obs, Jan 30, 1971

Obs, Jan 18, 1976

Obs, June 27, 1976

Obs, Sept 5, 1976

Obs, Nov 21, 1976

*Pompeii Exhibition opens
at the Royal Academy*

Obs, April 4, 1976

Obs, July, 1976

Summer heat beats all records

Obs, Feb 27, 1977

The Façade   Punch, Jan 10, 1973

'Redundant? Dammit, wait till King George hears of this!'   DM, July 18, 1969

Independent committee recommends plan to streamline Diplomatic Service

Join the UK and see the world   DM, Feb 11, 1970

Plight of would-be Asian-Indian immigrants

'I always knew they began at Calais'

Obs, Dec 1968

Obs, June 20, 1976

'A dark and ever menacing shadow...' – Enoch Powell, June 9, 1969

DM, June 11, 1969

...As worn by Enoch Powell   DM, Jan 19, 1970

Punch, June 20, 1973

Enoch Powell feeds the media

'They're asking for volunteers to go home!'   DM, April 10, 1968

Race riots in USA

'I sure hope they find another way of doing it.'   DM, April 9, 1969

opposite

DM, July 16, 1969   *President Nixon phones Apollo 11 astronauts before count-down*

'Now there's *real* progress – his father used to be a butler here.'   DM, April 30, 1969

White House dinner given for the Duke's 70th birthday

The shirt called PRIDE by Peter England

Daily Mail

BUDGET MONEY MAIL TODAY

NO. 22,999 WEDNESDAY, APRIL 15, 1970 PRICE 6d.

The hours of hope

Comment

So far and yet so near

NOW we see the true courage of the Moonmen. Our prayers are with their families. Our longing is for their safe return.

The tiny craft limping through space carries the hopes of mankind.

No man has ever been more alone than the three men cramped inside. No stranger has ever felt closer to our hearts.

TIDYING UP

MOST of what Mr Jenkins said yesterday was sensible. It's what he failed to say that worries us.

The Chancellor has avoided the temptation to buy easy popularity by reducing taxes on beer and cigarettes.

He has chosen instead to concentrate relief on the bottom end of the scale, on the people who didn't even pay income tax before Labour got in.

Inflation is the villain of the piece. Mr Jenkins has put up income tax allowances so that most of us, but particularly the very low paid and pensioners, get some compensation for rising prices and taxes.

The relief is pitifully small, about 3s. a week for most married couples. But better than nothing.

We are also glad to see Mr Jenkins using the welcome surplus on our balance of payments to pay back a large slice of the huge overseas debts which the Government ran up before and at the time of devaluation.

Mr Jenkins, cautious as ever, has tidied up the books. This is not an election Budget, but he has cleared the way for an election at any time.

Yet his caution is also depressing. For there is nothing in the Budget to *encourage* any of us to earn an extra pound or save an extra penny.

The Chancellor argues that the flood of wage rises makes this difficult. But the atmosphere of grab-what-you-can is the direct result of 5½ years of Labour government.

Throughout that time we have not had one single measure to spur us on.

The two most frequent complaints today are 'Why should I work any harder when the tax shoots up if I do overtime?' — and 'Why should I bother to save today when the money will be worth only half as much tomorrow?'

That is the malady of our times. And Mr Jenkins's quiet little Budget will not begin to cure it, any more than a peppermint pastille will cure a raging hangover.

From ANGUS MACPHERSON in HOUSTON, TEXAS

THE balance of life or death for the Apollo 13 astronauts in their ordeal aboard their stricken spacecraft depends on 20 gallons of water.

To come back safely they must ration themselves and their spacecraft to just under two pints of water an hour.

In the spacecraft water is used not only for drinking but also for cooling the electronic systems and the astronauts' cabin.

Without it the astronauts—Jim Lovell, Fred Haise and Jack Swigert—would be unable to protect themselves from the fierce heat of the sun or operate their instruments and engine for the vital manœuvres to bring them safely back.

When disaster struck the unlucky Apollo 13 the astronauts were already too close to the Moon to come home without at least one swing around it.

• Early today nerves at the Mission Control room in Houston were stretched taut as the spaceship hurtled towards the Moon before vanishing behind it for an agonising half-hour.

During that time the spacecraft was lost to the giant radar eyes tracking it from Earth

Space alarm Pages 8 and 9

240,000 miles away and out of all radio contact with Mission Control.

With the spacecraft out from behind the Moon and heading back towards Earth, the astronauts were due at 3.38 a.m. (BST) to use a blast of power lasting four minutes 20 seconds.

This would bring Apollo 13 down in the Pacific, 300 miles south of Samoa, between 6 p.m. and 7 p.m. on Friday.

The trouble began for the astronauts with a bang in the spaceship. Oxygen drained away from its service module, its main power section—oxygen which not only gives the astronauts air, but also provides all their electrical power by reacting with hydrogen in special cells.

The spacecraft's main 20,500lb-thrust engine was out of action because of the loss of all power in the mother ship Odyssey. So the astronauts had to rely on the engine of the lunar landing module Aquarius, still linked to Odyssey. But it has only half the power of the Odyssey unit.

Officials rejected a plan which would have brought the astronauts home earlier but which would have been more risky.

There was little conversation with the ground. The astronauts were told to cut their talk as much as possible to save power.

For more than an hour Houston control kept up a nonstop conversation with Lovell referring him to the instructions and data the astronauts had been given for emergency.

IN WASHINGTON the Senate yesterday called on all Americans to pause briefly at 9 p.m. to pray for the safe return of the astronauts.

IN BRITAIN ITV and BBC TV planned to stay on the air until 4 a.m. with Apollo coverage and Radios 1 and 2 broadcast throughout the night. BBC 1 will broadcast a special Apollo programme between 7 a.m. and 9 a.m. today.

Royal Navy ships were asked to stand by in case of a splashdown in the Indian Ocean.

The Budget that nearly wasn't

By WALTER TERRY, Political Editor

IT WAS a cautious, hedging, ever-so-careful Budget the Chancellor, Mr Roy Jenkins, produced yesterday—coffee, no cream, too many wafers and not enough ice cream. Hardly a vote winner for the General Election.

But it made gestures to the lower paid, old people and some surtax payers. After that—nothing spectacular.

There may be another Budget, with bigger tax cuts, just before the election.

Mr Jenkins hinted as much. 'If I find my judgment is too cautious it is much easier to correct this later in the year than if I go too fast,' he said.

Some Labour MPs asked last night: Has Roy put stern duty before vote-winning?

At a meeting of the Tories' back-bench finance committee Mr John Smith, MP for the Cities of London and Westminster, called it a 'bankers' Budget,' with Bank Rate cut, stamp duty off cheques and lending restrictions eased.

The Opposition leader, Mr Edward Heath, denounced it as a one-month Budget. All the tax benefits, amounting to more than £200 million, would be wiped out, he claimed, by a month's price increases in the shops.

Ruins

Sarcastically he congratulated Mr Jenkins on being the first Labour Chancellor since 1949 actually to cut taxes. There were only 17 Tories and 60 Labour MPs left in the Commons today who could truly sing: 'Twice in a lifetime.'

The Liberal Party's spokesman on economic affairs, Mr Richard Wainwright, said: 'The Budget speech was the blurred sound of a man buried in wreckage—the total ruins of incomes policy.

'The splendid fruits of the economic turnround had all been raided before the Chancellor spoke — by those powerful enough to force large pay rises.'

Labour MPs, pushing hard against a Tory lead in the country, with a General Election only months away, hoped Roy would set an exciting pace.

Studiously he did the opposite. Insistently he pointed to

Budget special Page SIX

the big success, a balance of payments surplus that should not be frittered away.

He made these claims for his third Budget: It will not put any prices up, no one will be worse off, two million will stop paying income tax altogether, and there will be benefits for 16,500,000 people.

Mr Jenkins called it 'a significant lightening of the burden' but admitted too, that he was deliberately cautious.

Bank Rate was reduced by ½ p.c. to 7 p.c.—down now to crisis rate, scoffed Mr Heath.

Borrowed money stays tight, except for exporters.

Politically Mr Jenkins can claim to have kept things simmering quietly until nearer the election, when, maybe, he will lower taxes on drink and tobacco.

The strategy seems to be: do it quietly and gently for the time being. Either the Treasury has fallen asleep, a big bang is coming, or the Cabinet is settling for a quiet stroll up to polling day.

THESE ARE THE MAIN CHANGES

TAX changes announced by Mr Jenkins give increased personal allowances but abolish the 6s. intermediate rate of tax. It means the vast majority of taxpayers—married men earning over £16 a week—are left with only 3s. a week more.

INCOME TAX: The single man's allowance jumps by £70 from £255 to £325, and the married allowance by £90 — £375 to £465.

But the reduced rate relief—under which the first £260 of taxable income is charged at 6s. in the £ instead of 8s. 3d.—disappears.

The changes free some two million people from income tax, mostly married couples. The concession starts now, but the effect on the pay packet will not be felt until the first pay-day after July 1.

Tax—nil

From £16 a week upwards a single man will pay 7s. 6d. *more* tax a year, but a married couple will pay £7 12s. 6d. a year less.

Examples:

Persons without children—Income £8 per week: Old tax £20, new tax nil.

Income £11: Old tax £57, new £49. Income £16: Old tax £132, new £132.

Married couples without children—income £11 p.w.: Old tax £21, new nil. Income £14: Old tax £57, new £41.

SURTAX: It will be charged only on surtaxable income exceeding £2,500 instead of £2,000, but will be payable at the same rates as at present—

Turn to Page 6, Col. 4

DAILY MAIL NORTHCLIFFE HOUSE, E.C.4 01-353 6000

LATE NEWS

DEATH TOLL IN BOMB BLAST

SAIGON: At least 20 Vietnamese civilians killed or injured by Viet Cong bomb blast in Central Saigon. Police said women hid explosive charge in parked motorcycle.

● WEATHER: Warmer. Details: Page NINE.

LATE WIRE — Best from Newmarket: SHINY TENTH (3.5, nap) and MEADOWVILLE (3.35).

4

Children swept into sea

LISBON: Six British children were swept into the sea by strong waves at Carcavelos, near Lisbon, while walking along the water's edge.

Local fishermen dashed into the water and pulled them out. One boy was taken to hospital. The children were members of a school party from the British India liner Uganda.

Record exports

Exports and imports hit new peaks in March as Britain's overseas trade balance showed a £5 million surplus for the month compared with a £7m. deficit in February.

City—PAGE 11

Law's long nose

BEIRUT: Chief, a two-year-old police dog from Britain, is Lebanon's latest weapon against hashish smugglers. He can sniff out the drug even when it is buried a foot in the ground.

New air link plan

Direct flights from London and Glasgow to Londonderry are planned to start in July.

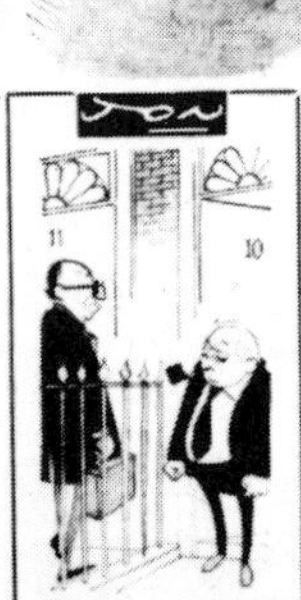

'Heaven knows what you'd have done if we'd been in the red.'

The £100 mayor

The new mayor of Folkestone, Kent, will cost the town £100 before he takes office. Mayor-elect Councillor John [illegible] is 6ft. 3in. and 16 stone and he will need a new and larger mayor's robe.

Train and fire engine in crash

A FIREMAN was killed and two of his colleagues were injured when a train and fire engine collided on an unmanned level crossing last night.

The eight-coach electric train, the 9.36 p.m. from Bishop's Stortford, Hertfordshire, to Liverpool Street, smashed the fire engine into a ditch when they met at the barrier crossing at Cadmore Lane, Cheshunt, Hertfordshire.

A police spokesman said last night that the firemen had unlocked the level-crossing barriers to get across. They had a key to the crossing, which was unmanned.

They were heading for a small fire on nearby marshes. 'It is thought to have been a waste fire and is now out,' said the spokesman.

No one in the train was injured.

The dead fireman was named as Sub-Officer Jim Bilton.

Marquis dies

Prince Philip's cousin and best man, the 50-year-old Marquis of Milford Haven, died last night, after collapsing at Liverpool Street Station, London, E.C.

(Obituary—Page THREE).

Decree for actor

Italian-born actress Yole Marinelli, 29, offered no defence in the London Divorce Court yesterday when her actor and photographer husband, Brian Weske, 38, was granted a decree nisi because of her adultery with actor Michael Elphick.

Wall Street

NEW YORK: Wall Street stock market closed lower but above the day's worst and the Dow Jones Industrial Index ended 3.14 down at 780.56. Trading volume jumped 2,040,000 shares to 10,850,000.

'No – it's *apart* from this one.'   DM, May 6, 1970

Ohio students shot dead in campus protest

One small step for man. . .   DM, May 8, 1970

opposite

After Dürer   DM, April 15, 1970

DM, May 27, 1970

American correspondent reports that force of student opinion has real power to affect policy

'After what we've done to it?'   DM, Mar 11, 1970

Red Indian civil rights demonstration to reclaim land at Fort Lawton, Seattle, as reservation

'You think I wouldn't like to throw mine away too?'   Punch, May 5, 1971

Ex-servicemen return their war medals

The Festival of the Eating of Words   Obs, Feb 27, 1972   *Nixon visits Peking*

Punch, April 5, 1972

America's Imperial Sunset

Punch cover, May 31, 1972

Punch, Nov 8, 1972

Americans weary of Vietnam involvement

'Now will you believe me when I say I'm too old to fight?'

'What do you mean, not very Christmassy – they don't have Christmas.'   Obs, Dec 24, 1972

US air offensive against North Vietnam

Obs, Jan 28, 1973
Ceasefire in Vietnam

'You don't think it could be misunderstood?'   Obs, May 6, 1973
Watergate burglaries revealed

Punch, June 13, 1973

Watergate continued

'It can't be for me – I'm the Sheriff.'

Punch, July 4, 1973

'...And for my next trick...'   Punch, July 25, 1973

'Jump!'   Punch, Nov 14, 1973

Watergate continued

Obs.

Obs, June 30, 1974

Punch, Dec 11, 1974

Ford and Brezhnev summit talks at Vladivostok agree arms limitation

Obs, Mar 9, 1975

Behind every great man. . .   Obs, July 18, 1976

Democratic Party nominates Jimmy Carter as Presidential candidate

Carter's America   Punch cover, Jan 19, 1977

'Freedom from what?'

The only good Jew is a dead one?

DM, Jan 29, 1969

Obs, June 6, 1971

Journey's End   Punch, June 27, 1973

Trial Run   Punch, Sept 12, 1973

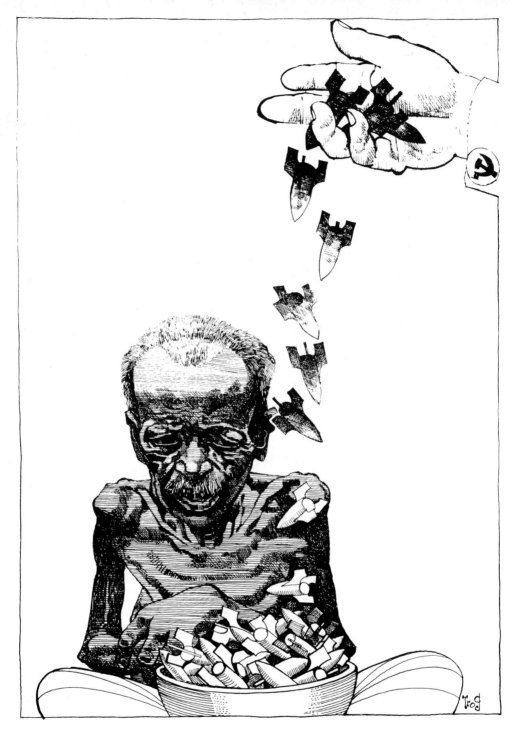

'To each according to his needs' – Karl Marx   Punch, Nov 13, 1974

'Subversive *horses*?'

Obs, Sept 9, 1973

European 3-day event in Kiev

'Peace, my children.'   DM, Jan 3, 1969

Russia steps up Middle East peace bid as Israeli forces mass on Lebanon border

DM, Jan 10, 1969

Arab fears increase at reports of Israeli secret bomb

'When Dr Kissinger and Mr Le Duc Tho arrived at agreement
on an armistice after three years of difficult negotiations,
a wave of joy and hope for peace surged through the world' –
from the 1973 Nobel Peace Prize citation.

Punch, Oct 24, 1973

opposite

Punch, Sept 13, 1972

Arab terrorist attack at the Munich Olympics

Which Doctor?　　Obs, May 2, 1976

Punch, July 18, 1974

INSIDE EVERY FAT MAN...

...THERE IS A THIN MAN TRYING TO GET OUT

Punch, Sept 15, 1971

Lord Goodman conducts Rhodesia talks

' "Ye can tell a man that boozes
By the company he chooses."
At that, the pig got up and walked away!'

Relations between Smith and Vorster cool

Obs, Jan 30, 1977

Bullock Report recommends workers' participation at board level

Punch, Feb 2, 1977

The White Lions
'It is not expected that the white lions recently discovered
in Southern Africa will survive for very long, since their
colour means that they are totally unequipped for dealing with
their environment'– BBC News

Punch, May 18, 1977

'So, Al Capone had car crashes, too.'   Obs, Feb 27, 1977

The Archbishop of Uganda's death reported 'in a car crash' after his arrest in Kampala

He who rides a tiger. . .   DM, Jan 30, 1969

Ian Paisley injures hand in police fracas while having a warrant served upon him

'It's just as well they believe in the same God.'   DM, Aug 20, 1969

'No bombing tonight, Paddy – too bloody light.'   Punch, Dec 22, 1971

Temporary Christmas truce declared by IRA bombers

A Lick and a Promise   Punch, June 7, 1972

Official IRA announces suspension of terrorist operations

'Heathen bloody savages!'   Punch, Sept 27, 1972

The Queen's Silver Jubilee
1977

Obs, June 12, 1977